Treasures of the Heart

Oliver Forward

Treasures of the Heart
Copyright © 2024 by Oliver Forward

ISBN: 979-8895310311 (hc)
ISBN: 979-8895310298 (sc)
ISBN: 979-8895310304 (e)

All rights reserved. No part of this publication may be reproduced, distributed, or transmitted in any form or by any means, including photocopying, recording, or other electronic or mechanical methods, without the prior written permission of the publisher and/or the author, except in the case of brief quotations embodied in critical reviews and other noncommercial uses permitted by copyright law.

The views expressed in this book are solely those of the author and do not necessarily reflect the views of the publisher, and the publisher hereby disclaims any responsibility for them.

Writers' Branding
(877) 608-6550
www.writersbranding.com
media@writersbranding.com

Contents

Oh, My Arm Candy 1

Silence Has Become the Wings of My Thoughts 2

I've Been Lost in Time 3

A Distinguished Gentleman 4

Are You So Unhappy 6

Beauty Is When 7

Bye-Bye Dreams 8

Can I, My Love 9

Come Into My World of Hair 10

How Can You 11

I Can Taste Your Love 12

I Can't Sleep Without Your Love 13

I Love You 14

I Love You More Than Myself 15

I Miss You Already 16

I Want to Escape 17

I'm So in Love With You 18

Music to My Tears 19

If Only I Had Wings 21

Still, It Does Not Matter 22

The Curtain of My Heart Has Broken 23

This Love 24

Waiting 25

When the Pain Is Gone 26

Why Am I Dying for Your Kiss? 27

You Mean More to Me Than a Friend 28

Your Lips Deserve It 29

You're Like a Mirror in My Mind 30

You're So Beautiful 31

Oh, My Arm Candy

Oh, my arm candy I love you so much

My love, I do not have a future without you

Without you all these years,

I still lock my eyes like closed curtains every time we kiss

There is no defense against your seducing love

I find it very hard functioning in life without you

Only if you live inside of me

Oh, my arm candy

I want to be the main character in your favorite dream

Because of my love for you, many beautiful flowers die as a token of my love for you

Oh, my arm candy

This passionate love I have for you is the most powerful feeling in the world

So amazing, your love is running through my heart as if it was a prosthetic heart designed only for your touch

I feel the greatest symphony running inside my heartbeats every time your consuming electrifying lips press against mine

I can hear the stars' explosion under the moonlight

Oh, my arm candy!

Silence Has Become the Wings of My Thoughts

Silence has become the wings of my thoughts
I'm hearing things that are not there
Your voice seems to walk up and down in the pocket of my mind
Like a wild stallion running across an open prairie, unbridled and free
Your kindness has boxed me inside the canyon of your adorable arms
Yes, my love, silence has become the wings of my thoughts
The impact of your love is stronger than that of intoxicating wine
Being away from you, I feel so insecure
Every moment without you, for sure, defines eternity
Every vein in my body carries your love
Like a ship carrying cargo across the Atlantic Sea
Silence has become the wings of my thoughts.

I've Been Lost in Time

I've been lost in time

You are like an intercom that keeps sounding in my mind

Your beautiful eyes keep melting my heart like the wax from a burning candle

I shake my head only to break away from daydreaming

Every time you touch me, you send electric shocks through my body

I can feel your eyes like arrows piercing into the side of my head

I find it so utterly impossible to keep my hands to myself

You're so inviting

You are the perfect example of what life is all about

I have the strongest appetite to love you before the sunrise

I promised you that I would love you till the end of time

The idea of letting you go could never cross my mind

You are everything to me

With you, I feel so complete

Even the stars of heaven bow at your feet

I've been lost in time.

A Distinguished Gentleman

A distinguished gentleman, so full of grace down through the years, you have been instrumental in changing lives.

Admired by many and still cherishing your wife, with things being in perspective, a legend you became.

As you have taken your call seriously, to you, life is not a game.

A person who has taken in so many under your wings is because of you that some now desire to be queens and kings.

The decades that you mentored were not in vain; from it so many have benefited, and many have gained

The public has been served in a distinguished Manner, your professionalism had indeed been "one of a kind", as men of your caliber are not easy to find.

If someone compared you to a needle in a haystack, how accurate would they be? Precise as can be since there's not many like you.

Always tending to stand out in the crowd because your life speaks volumes, and it should make your people proud.

You have helped so many to reach fame that some are mesmerized when they hear your name.

Like the clouds that are pended to the sky, what you have produced will never die.

You have shared a legacy that is worth living by.

Up to now, your life has been what others are dreaming that theirs will be, for you have laid the foundation of a real visionary

The world knows you as a man who has been leaving your mark as you go through life teaching others how to live

People from all walks of life are being touched by that elegant tone of voice that you have, which is filled with powerful magic

You are such a skillful speaker

As you journey through life amazingly, you have remained meek

A living legend, you have traveled many roads, distances both near and far

Many people have been inspired by your life and career

You have gained many assets in your days of preaching, teaching, and reaching. You have possessions that will always mean so much.

They will forever be treasured by those whose lives you have touched

In the Thomas F. Freeman building, as you walk the halls, there are thousands of pictures hanging on the tall walls.

Your staff and debate team have left so many trophies for the world to see a legend's trail of victory.

You have made so many normal lives become extraordinary.

An honor only you can carry. Your mind is build like a monastery

Your voice has inspired thousands of students to achieve in a system that has incarcerated many.

You have successfully taught boys and girls to become exceptionally men and women in a changing world

You have lived this life like a flag blowing through the turbulence of the winds, always being surrounded by so many loyal friends.

You have left an everlasting impression on so many.

You have set the pace of a distinguished gentleman ... so full of grace.

Are You So Unhappy

Are you so unhappy that you can live your life without me?
I tried my best not to love you as much, but with no success
Would you explain to me so I could see this shouldn't be?
You're living inside my dreams
There is water in my face every morning;
I wake up to a wet pillowcase
The grip of love won't release me
Your footprints of love keep walking across the shadows of my mind
Are you so unhappy?

Beauty Is When

The true definition of beauty is when a woman's heart has been turned inside out

Beauty is when you meet a man for the first time, and his eyes take a three-second nap at high noon

Beauty is when you are under the moonlight and a man looks into your eyes

And your heart shows up, and all he can do is cry

Beauty is when a person falls in love with lust and connects with true love

Beauty is when you are misunderstood by those who are seeking everlasting passion

Beauty is a vision locked within the distance of an eagle's eye

Beauty is when you frame one's face and hang it in the middle of your soul

Beauty is when you are under control in slow motion and yet put a timer on the movement

Beauty is thoughtfulness while being admired

Beauty is priceless even though you have picked the right Mega-Ball

Beauty is more powerful than any Powerball

Beauty is when…

Bye-Bye Dreams

My dreams seem to be my life
But sometimes, they get shattered
My dreams are my only designated home
I live alone and trust my love because it is so strong
Yet sometimes I don't understand why my dreams fall out my hand
I gave my love and flew like a dove
Now, my happiness and joy have been destroyed
I thought I had found the perfect lover
Sad to say
This one was just like the other
My heart has been broken and put to shame
I feel like life has beaten me with a chain
This pain is as painful as a sharp, cold knife
Like a woman's womb in reverse
The blood runs in, not out
Like a water's tide
Yet I survive
Bye-bye, my dreams.

Can I, My Love

Can I, my love, tell you how much I love you?

Can I, my love, stare into your captivating eyes?

Can I, my love, climb over your perfect radius chin only to fall into your fountain of love?

Can I, my love, kiss you until I cry?

Can I, my love, sleep tonight between your twin-towered breasts?

Can I, my love, taste the liquid spice of your love?

Can I, my love? Can I?

Come Into My World of Hair

The greatest styles your eyes have ever seen
Come into my world of hair
Inside it, you will see magic styles that make the ladies and men smile
Do not be afraid
And do not be shy
When I am finished
Just watch people's eyes as you walk by
It may be cut short
To shine and smile at the sun
Again, it may be silky and long
To blow with the wind
My clippers make a buzzing sound
Wanting to put my styles all over town
My scissors clip into the empty thin air
Thinking about the styles they want to share
Come into my world of hair
Let us have a hair affair
Come into my world of hair
Where hair falls in love with styles
Where people can wear their clothes proud
Use your mind
As clouds flow in the sky
You can have these styles as they pass by
Come into my world of hair.

How Can You

How can you cut your love off like a light switch on the wall?

Knowing I'm in love with you

To live in this world without your love

I'll just stumble and fall

I can't help the fact that I'm so in love with you

I'll love you forever, my love

As long as I shall live

Your love has become my alarm clock

That reminds me to embrace you every hour of the day

Tell me, my love,

How can you cut your love off?

This deep battle of passion keeps burning through me

Like fire consuming a field of dry sage

How am I supposed to pass this love test?

Without you, I can never find rest

How can you?

I Can Taste Your Love

I can taste your love
Slipping through my lips
Even though I have not had the pleasure of kissing you today
Each day is always special to me
I can truly feel your love draining from the bottom of my soul
Just last night
You placed your lips upon mine and kissed them repeatedly until they were left so tender
I felt your love reconstructing my abandoned heart
Thank you for loving me back to life
You've met me at my weakest point
I had no other choice but to fall in love with you
I really can taste your love slipping through my lips
You will always belong in my heart
You are so beautiful
When you are not around, I feel so alone
Yet, at times, you still seem to be so near
I can hear footsteps walking across the clouds
To the hallways of my mind
As the rolling tide leaps from the boisterous sea,
Yes, the story of two lovers kissing on the ocean pier
It is a love scene to see
I can feel the gentle breeze blowing across our skin
Again, I can really taste your love slipping through my lips.

I Can't Sleep Without Your Love

I can't sleep without your love
I'm so cold on the outside and freezing inside
All because you're not by my side
Like a lion would patiently lay and capture its prey
I wish there were a way I could capture your heart
When you're not near, it tears me apart
Every love affair needs a brand-new start
Believe me, my life, I can't sleep without your love
Again, I'm so cold on the outside and freezing inside
All because you're not by my side
Every time I close my eyes, I can see only your face
Believe me, my love, I can't sleep without your love
Again, I'm so cold on the outside and freezing inside
I can't make it another night without you
Things just don't seem right
All the good moments we have had together
I can't sleep without your love.

I Love You

I love you for your looks

I love you for your smile

I love you for your pity that keeps my eyes dry

I love you for your comfort as long as you stand by

I love you perhaps more than I could say

I love you for the time you look at me

I love you like a fish loves the sea

I love you through eternity

I love you so much that I've lost my sight

I love you!

I love you!

I Love You More Than Myself

I love you so much that every moment without you reminds me how the stars feel in the day

Knowing that it's so difficult when the sun is smiling

It seems almost impossible to waiting on midnight

My imagination has drained so much energy

I can't relinquish these thoughts I have for you

My dreams have become nightmares

I'm lost inside of you

And I can't find my way out

The trail of love has taken me to my love

I don't want to go back home alone

I've put your love on the bookshelf of my heart

I love you more than I love myself.

I Miss You Already

I miss you already

For the sun has fallen asleep like a weeping willow of Babylon

Now I'm experiencing lonely teardrops

Falling to the basement of my lonely soul

Please don't leave me gazing into space without you

I feel so out of place

My world has completely changed now

How can I survive life without you

I haven't the slightest clue

It's going to be difficult not seeing your beautiful face

I miss you already

What am I to do without your love?

You're always on my mind

My love for you was unconditional

I appreciate everything about you

Being in love with you now, I must steer myself away from you

I never thought this would happen to me

When you went your way, I died inside

You took the other side with you

I miss you already.

I Want to Escape

I want to escape from your love

But I can't

I am fascinated by the qualities you possess

I'm so excited about the time

Even when you're not around

It seems so easy for my tears to run free

I can hear the echoes of your silent love

Dancing deep down against the hollow walls of my empty soul

Oh, my love

I miss you

I realize that I can't pretend anymore

Honestly, I really love you.

I'm So in Love With You

Last night, in my sleep

I turned over

To wrap my arms around you

But you were not there

This deep loneliness caused me to cry out

For your love

I searched everywhere

You could not be found

Relief only came when I started tracing my tears back to my heart

I'm so in love with you.

Music to My Tears

My silent tears are proof that they are just silent rhythms to be written into Music

That governs the melody of the amplifier of my heart

My tears gave birth to the piano and named the black and white keys

Music to my tears, Music to my tears!

Music to my tears, Music to my tears!

My tears gave birth to the trumpet, so we hear the warning sounds blowing, letting us know that time on the earth will not exist anymore

Music to my tears, Music to my tears!

Music to my tears, Music to my tears!

My tears gave birth to the flute and put different imprints on the holes so the thumb and fingers could have control, letting the music move the soul

Music to my tears, Music to my tears!

Music to my tears, Music to my tears!

My tears gave birth to the violin; after the bow ravished the strings, a loud scream was made, and a melody was born

Music to my tears, Music to my tears!

Music to my tears, Music to my tears!

My tears gave birth to the saxophone, only to shake our bones like a newborn baby crying in a crib and causing the spine to shake with cold chills

Music to my tears, Music to my tears!

Music to my tears, Music to my tears!

My tears gave birth to the lead guitar and put the tenor sound in the strings and the chords and the riffs into the words that turned into myths

Music to my tears, Music to my tears!

Music to my tears, Music to my tears!

My tears gave birth to the drumsticks that put the pacemaker bass inside the drums

Music to my tears, Music to my tears!

Music to my tears, Music to my tears!

My tears gave birth to the tear glands so my nervous system could be aroused

Music to my tears, Music to my tears!

Music to my tears, Music to my tears!

If Only I Had Wings

I've been touched by your love
The perpetual shadows of your love
Won't leave me alone
I really love you today
More than ever before
If only I had wings
To soar high through the sky
Searching for a place to land
Hopefully, upon your sweet cranberry lips
To drink the moist from your wet kisses
If only I had wings!

Still, It Does Not Matter

Still, it does not matter

I do not like the fact that we are not talking

I feel so alone at times

I cry sheets of pain when you're not around

I feel so down

Still, it does not matter

If you go, I want you to know I will always love you through eternity

I can't live without you

I think about you day and night

But most of the time

When the night rolls around

I feel hopeless

Oftentimes, it seems so unfair

Being in love all by myself

Still, it does not matter.

The Curtain of My Heart Has Broken

The curtain of my heart has broken

Now I'm left alone in the dark

Someone, please, please call my love so I can see you again

The silent echoes are writhing against the thin walls of my eardrum

I feel so handicapped

My loneliness is yelling at me

There is no comfort living life without you

I feel like I'm lost in space

This hurt seems to dominate my thoughts and reactions

Please, my love, would you call?

I hate being alone

Come back into my life

And be the sun in this dark place

Listen, how can you say we can only be friends knowing

I'm in love with you?

The curtain of my heart has broken.

This Love

So profound when I found out that you loved me
Your expression exposes the ultimate truths
I want to love you back
The day I laid eyes on you
How elegant and refined you were
I wanted you to become my soul mate
This love I have for you has enslaved me
I am eagerly waiting for intimacy
This love!

Waiting

Your absence tells me how much I love you
Your Botox lips force me to feel the love
You have found the entrance to my waiting heart
You make me live my dream
This moment of waiting defined my love for you
Surrounded by this foreign emotion
You have enslaved me
Waiting for the opportunity to love you
From the depths of my heart
In the meantime
Let's just exchange kisses
While waiting.

When the Pain Is Gone

When the pain is gone, there is no one else to blame

When the pain is gone, there are no more empty days

When the pain is gone, there is no more loneliness

When the pain is gone, there is no more guiltiness

When the pain is gone, there is no more sadness

When the pain is gone, there is no reason to cry

When the pain is gone, there is a reason to move on

When the pain is gone….

Why Am I Dying for Your Kiss?

Kiss me if you love me

Kiss me so I will never be sad

Kiss me because the safety valve of my heart has been broken

So, therefore, I cry, "Kiss me."

Before my tears become like a floodgate and put out my fire

Kiss me as if it was the very first time

Kiss me before I lose my mind

Kiss me and prove to my heart your love is true

Kiss me so that my lips may hold onto your sweet cherry tongue

Kiss me so I may hold you close

Kiss me, and I promise never to let you go

Kiss me, oh, my love, all through the night

Kiss me and at the same time embrace me tight

Kiss me, my darling, until the break of night

Will you kiss me?

You Mean More to Me Than a Friend

You mean more to me than a friend

The love I have for you I can't end

I keep asking myself, why do love goodbyes always hurt so bad?

My love for you has made me ecstatic

Without you, I'll just go insane

Knowing I can't live through the pain

You know everything about me

Even my level of love

I can't imagine loving anyone else

I'm in love with you

The tear gate of my soul has dried up

There's nothing extra left inside of me

But only your love footprints that are deep in my soul

You mean more to me than a friend.

Your Lips Deserve It

My heart is boiling over to love you

What an emotional shift you have brought into my life

I'm honored to be in love with you

What a celebration of love locked inside of me

I have been captured by your precious sensibility

You're so classic

I have been lured by your love

My heart is racing so fast; I really want you

Come, come closer

I want to kiss you

Come closer

I want to kiss you

Your lips deserve it.

You're Like a Mirror in My Mind

When you are away from me
You're like a mirror in my mind
Every time I close my eyes, I see you all the time
You're like a mirror in my mind
The reflection of your smile has full control over me
You're like a mirror in my mind
Your salty tears have left stains on my glass heart
You're like a mirror in my mind
Forever, we'll be lost in time
You're like a mirror in my mind
Every time I close my eyes, I see you all the time
You're like a mirror in my mind.

You're So Beautiful

I've always known that I should fall in love with you

However, for you to fall in love with me, no

Never have I ever met a woman like you

You, your personality is totally new

I was surprised when I took that look into your pretty brown eyes

That hair of yours is dark as the night

And your teeth shine like pearls

I would have to say you are my dream girl

Those dimples in your jaw make me observe the sugar-brown skin

That looks as warm and soft as if it would sparkle under the moonlight

To me, you are so beautiful

That I cannot even imagine

You are so beautiful.

www.ingramcontent.com/pod-product-compliance
Lightning Source LLC
LaVergne TN
LVHW041601070526
838199LV00046B/2090